WITHDRAWN

EARTH, SPACE, AND BEYOND

WHAT DO WE KNOW ABOUT
THE SOLAR SYSTEM?

Ian Graham

Chicago, Illinois

www.heinemannraintree.com
Visit our website to find out
more information about
Heinemann-Raintree books.

To order:
 Phone 888-454-2279
Visit www.heinemannraintree.com
to browse our catalog and order online.

© 2011 Raintree
an imprint of Capstone Global Library, LLC
Chicago, Illinois

Visit our website at
www.heinemannraintree.com

All rights reserved. No part of this publication may be
reproduced or transmitted in any form or by any means,
electronic or mechanical, including photocopying,
recording, taping, or any information storage and
retrieval system, without permission in writing from
the publisher.

Edited by Andrew Farrow, Adam Miller, and Adrian
Vigliano
Designed by Marcus Bell
Original illustrations ©Capstone Global Library 2011
Illustrated by KJA-artists.com
Picture research by Hannah Taylor
Originated by Capstone Global Library Ltd.
Printed and bound in the United States of America by
Corporate Graphics in North Mankato, Minnesota.
15 14 13 12 11
10 9 8 7 6 5 4 3 2 1

Library of Congress Cataloging-in-Publication Data
Cataloging-in-Publication Data is on file at the Library of
Congress.

ISBNs: 978-1-4109-4179-4 (HC) 978-1-4109-4185-5 (PB)

Acknowledgments
The author and publishers are grateful to the following
for permission to reproduce copyright material: Corbis
pp. 14 (©epa/Dennis M. Sabangan), 19 (©NASA), 35
(©Roger Ressmeyer), 36 (©Mike Agliolo), 38 (©Charles
O'Rear); NASA pp. 9, 11 (ESA/ CXC, JPL-Caltech, J. Hester
and A. Loll (Arizona State Univ.), R. Gehrz (Univ. Minn.),
and STScI), 12, 13, 15 (Goddard Space Flight Center
Scientific Visualization Studio), 16, 18 (ESA/ I. de Pater,
and M. Wong [UC Berkeley]), 20, 21 (JPL/ University of
Arizona), 24, 28 (JPL), 29 (PIRL / University of Arizona),
31 top, 31 bot, 33, 37 (JPL), 39 (JPL/Cornell), 39 (JPL/
Cornell), 41; Science Photo Library pp. 4-5 (©NASA/
JPL), 6 (©Lynette Cook), 7 (©Take 27 Ltd), 8 (©Gavin
Kingcome), 10 (©Mark Garlick), 23 (©Mark Garlick),
25 (©John Sanford), 27 (©Paul Wootton), 26 (©Pekka
Parvianinen), 30, 32 (©NASA), 34 (©Walter Pacholka,
Astropics), 40 (©John Chumack); shutterstock p. 17
(©corepics).

Cover photograph of Earth and the Moon orbiting the
Sun reproduced with permission of Science Photo Library
(© Steve Munsinger).

We would like to thank Professor George W. Fraser for his
invaluable help in the preparation of this book.

Disclaimer
All the Internet addresses (URLs) given in this book were
valid at the time of going to press. However, due to the
dynamic nature of the Internet, some addresses may
have changed, or sites may have changed or ceased to
exist since publication. While the author and publisher
regret any inconvenience this may cause readers, no
responsibility for any such changes can be accepted by
either the author or the publisher.

EARTH, SPACE, AND BEYOND

WHAT DO WE KNOW ABOUT THE SOLAR SYSTEM?

Contents

Some words are shown in bold, **like this**. You can find out what they mean by looking in the glossary. You can also look out for them in the "Word Station" box at the bottom of each page.

Our Solar System

We can see the stars in the night sky. Everyone knows something about Earth, the Sun, and the **Moon**. But how much do we really know about the **solar system**?

The basics

The solar system is made up of the Sun, the eight planets that **orbit** (circle around) it, and their moons. (Moons are small, rocky objects that orbit planets.) It includes everything that travels through space with them. The solar system is in constant motion. The planets spin and orbit the Sun. Moons spin and orbit most of the planets. Pieces of rock and ice fly around the Sun.

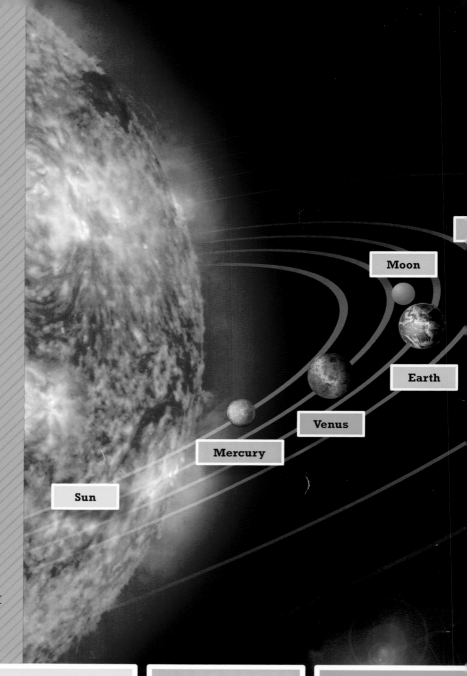

Moon

Earth

Venus

Mercury

Sun

Sun
The Sun is a star. It looks bigger and brighter than other stars because it is much closer to us.

Mercury
Mercury is the smallest planet in the solar system. It is just over one-third the size of Earth.

Venus
Venus is almost the same size as Earth. But its surface is hidden under thick clouds.

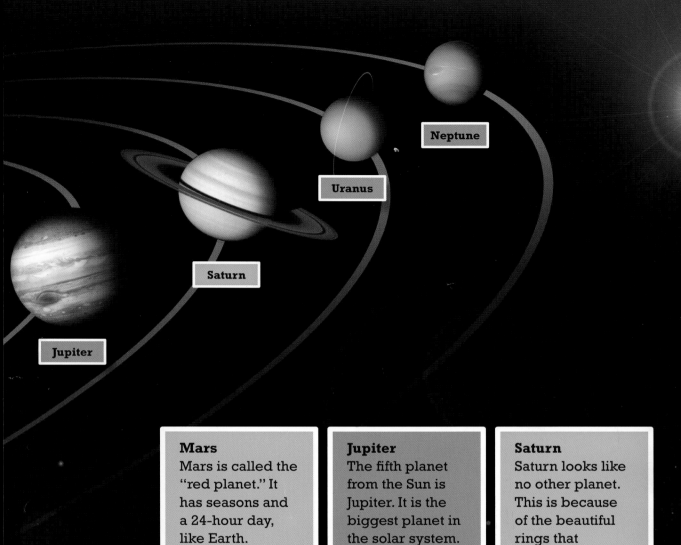

Neptune

Uranus

Saturn

Jupiter

Mars
Mars is called the "red planet." It has seasons and a 24-hour day, like Earth.

Jupiter
The fifth planet from the Sun is Jupiter. It is the biggest planet in the solar system.

Saturn
Saturn looks like no other planet. This is because of the beautiful rings that surround it.

Earth
Earth is unique. It is the only planet with liquid (flowing) water on its surface. It is the only planet where life is known to exist.

The Moon
Earth's Moon is the fifth-largest moon in the solar system. The Moon is about a quarter of the size of Earth.

Uranus
Uranus was the first planet to be discovered.

Neptune
Neptune is 30 times farther from the Sun than Earth. It has the fastest winds in the solar system.

WORD STATION
orbit circle around something, such as a planet

Where Did the Solar System Start?

The **solar system** was once a huge, swirling cloud of **gas** and dust. (A gas is a substance with no shape, like air.) This cloud is called a **nebula**. The Sun and planets did not exist.

A collapsing cloud

Nearly five billion years ago, the nebula began to collapse. The collapse may have been triggered by an exploding star. As the nebula fell in on itself, it started spinning faster. The spinning motion made the nebula flatten.

More than four billion years ago, the newly formed Sun was surrounded by dust like this.

WORD STATION
nebula cloud of dust and gas in space

As Earth formed, it was hit by billions of boulders.

Particles (tiny pieces) of dust in the nebula bumped into each other. Some stuck together, forming clumps. The biggest clump formed in the middle of the nebula. It became **denser** (more filled with material) and hotter. Over time, it formed the Sun.

Clumps of particles went on to form large boulders. As these boulders crashed into each other, this formed bigger bodies, called **protoplanets**. Protoplanets continued to crash into each other. They also grew by bringing in gas and dust. Over time, protoplanets formed the planets we see today.

You have weight because gravity pulls you down against the ground.

The pull of gravity

Gravity is like an invisible glue holding the **solar system** together. Gravity is the pull that a large object has on a smaller one nearby. The Sun has the strongest pull of gravity of any object in the solar system. So,the Sun's gravity keeps the planets circling in **orbits** around it.

Body matters

Earth has strong gravity, too. It pulls things toward the center of the planet—including us! Our muscles and bones have to be strong enough to overcome gravity. This is what allows us to stand up.

But in space, **astronauts** (people who travel to space in spacecraft) no longer feel the effects of gravity. This affects their bodies. During a space flight, astronauts' muscles become smaller. Their bones become weaker. Astronauts who go on very long space flights have to do at least two hours of exercise every day in space. This slows down these changes. When they come back to Earth, they feel the pull of gravity again. Their muscles and bones slowly return to normal strength.

Quick weight loss tip: Move to the Moon!

Your weight depends on the strength of gravity wherever you are. The **Moon's** gravity is weaker than Earth's. If you traveled to the Moon, you would weigh one-sixth as much as you do on Earth. Weaker gravity would let you jump higher, too.

bungee cord

Astronaut Nicole Stott exercises on a treadmill inside a spacecraft. Elastic bungee cords pull her down. They help stop her from floating away.

What is the solar system made of?

The **solar system** is made of **elements**. Elements are the simplest substances that exist. The elements **hydrogen** and **helium** have been around since the **universe** (space and everything in it) formed. That was 13.5 billion years ago.

Over time, the largest stars in the universe blew up in huge explosions called **supernovae**. These sprayed elements into space. In time, the remains of these dead stars were swept up. They became part of giant clouds called **nebulae**. As we have seen, these clouds formed the planets and other parts of our solar system. They were full of these sprayed elements.

We are here because of stars that exploded billions of years ago. These stars threw the building materials for our solar system into space.

The Crab Nebula is a cloud of gas and dust. It was thrown out by a supernova about 1,000 years ago.

We are made of stardust

Thanks to the elements in stardust, life on Earth exists. For example, humans are made of elements. Stars also made the element **oxygen** that we breathe. It made the element **nitrogen** that makes up most of the rest of Earth's **atmosphere**. The atmosphere is the layer of **gases** that surrounds our planet.

Why does the Sun shine?

The Sun looks like a burning ball of **gas**. But it does not burn like a fire. Instead, the Sun uses a process called **nuclear fusion** (see page 13).

Glowing gas hangs above the Sun's surface. This is called a **prominence**.

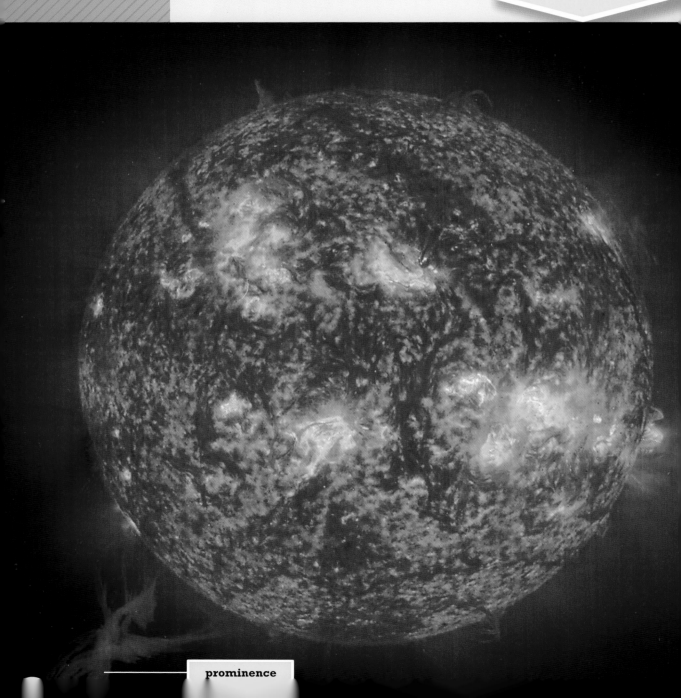

prominence

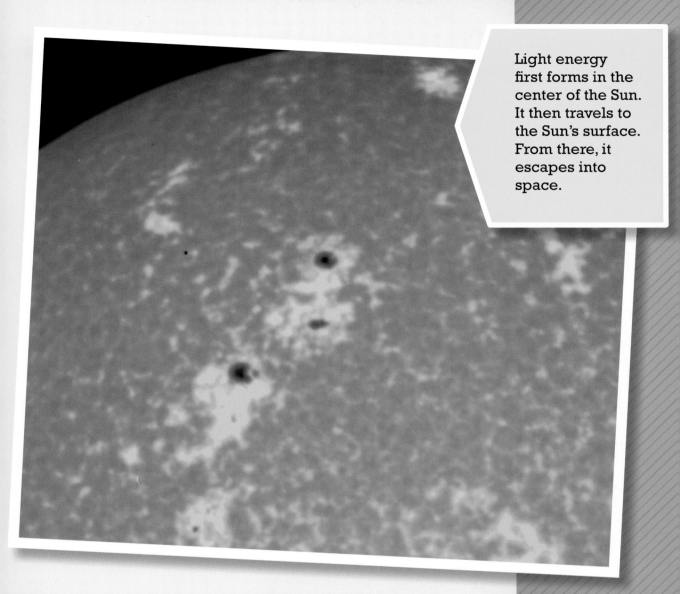

Light energy first forms in the center of the Sun. It then travels to the Sun's surface. From there, it escapes into space.

The Sun is made mainly of the **element hydrogen**. The temperature in the Sun's center is an amazing 15 million degrees Celsius (27 million Fahrenheit). At this temperature, hydrogen **atoms** are ripped apart. (Atoms are tiny building blocks that make up elements.) The pressure within the Sun then rejoins atoms. This rejoining forms a new element—**helium**.

This process of joining atoms this way is nuclear fusion. It releases **energy**, or the ability to do work. It makes the Sun shine.

The Family of Planets

The planets of the **solar system** all formed from the same cloud of **gas** and dust. But they are all very different. There are two main groups of planets.

The two groups of planets

The first group is made up of the small, **rocky planets** closest to the Sun. These include Mercury, Venus, Earth, and Mars. They all are built in a similar way. For example, on Earth, the ground we live on is a thin **crust**, or layer, of rock. This floats on Earth's surface. Beneath the crust, there is a layer of hot, liquid rock. This is called the **mantle**. It goes all the way down to Earth's **core**, or center. The core is a ball of metal.

The second group of planets is made up of planets called the **gas giants**. They include Jupiter, Saturn, Uranus, and Neptune. These planets lie far out in the solar system. Each gas giant has a small, solid core. This is surrounded by liquid and gas.

Villages often develop on the slopes of volcanoes. This is because the soil around volcanoes is very good for growing food.

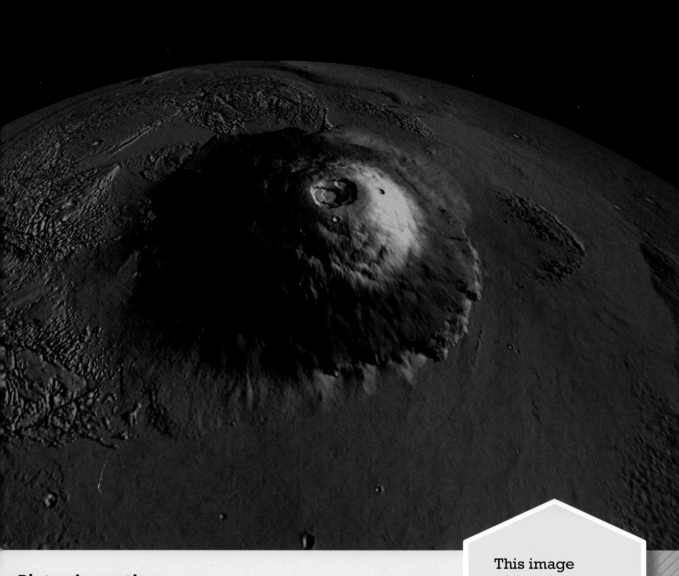

Plates in motion

Earth's crust is cracked into seven major **plates**, or sections, of rock. There are also 12 smaller sections. The plates move and rub against each other. They often catch and get stuck. When they spring free, the result is an earthquake. Hot rock melts up through the crust, near the edges of the plates. The hot rock and gases shoot out through volcanoes, which are openings in the crust.

This image of the planet Mars shows the biggest volcano in the solar system, Olympus Mons. A computer made the colors appear this way.

mantle melted rock layer of a planet lying between its core and crust

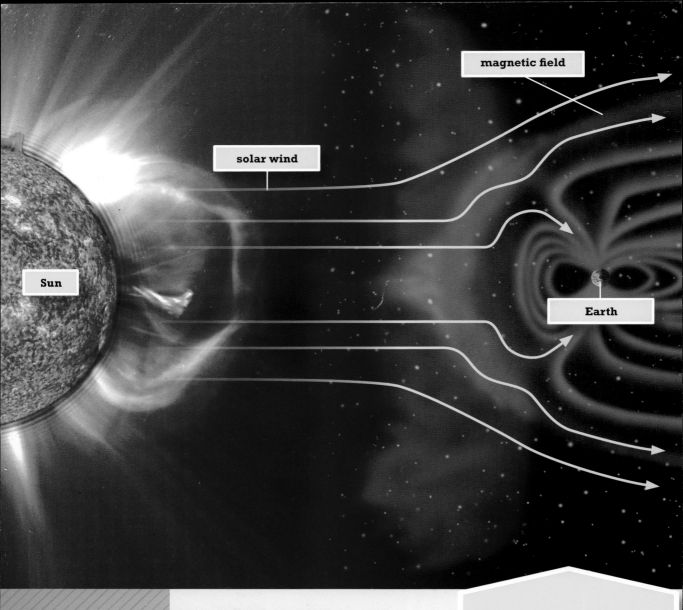

magnetic field

solar wind

Sun

Earth

Magnetic worlds

Earth behaves like a magnet, pulling things toward it. It is **magnetic**. This effect is created by its metal **core**. The **rocky planets** are not all magnetic in the way that Earth is. But the **gas giants**—Jupiter, Saturn, Uranus, and Neptune—have strong magnetic effects.

Earth's magnetic field keeps the solar wind away from Earth's surface.

WORD STATION
solar wind constant stream of particles flying out of the Sun

Lights in the sky

Earth's core creates a **magnetic field** around the planet. This acts like an invisible layer protecting Earth. The Sun constantly produces a stream of tiny material called **particles**. This constant flow of particles from the Sun is called the **solar wind**. The layer around Earth acts like a shield. It pushes away solar wind particles.

When the solar wind particles crash into Earth's protective layer, they give out light. Trillions of these crashes sometimes occur. This produces sheets of glowing colors in the sky. This light display is called an **aurora**.

The sky over northern Canada is lit up by an aurora.

Atmospheres

A planet's **atmosphere** is the layer of **gases** that surrounds it. The planet Mercury has almost no atmosphere at all. The planet Venus has a very thick atmosphere. Earth has a thick atmosphere, too. The planet Mars has a very thin atmosphere. All of the **gas giants** have thick atmospheres.

The atmospheres of the planets are made of different gases. Earth's atmosphere is mainly **nitrogen** and **oxygen** gas. We need oxygen to breathe and live. The atmosphere also shields us from harmful **energy** from the Sun. It spreads the Sun's warmth around the planet.

Planets with atmospheres have weather. The weather we experience on Earth happens in the lowest layer of the atmosphere, closest to Earth's surface. This is called the **troposphere**. On Jupiter, a huge storm has been raging for hundreds of years.

Jupiter's Great Red Spot is a giant storm. It has been spinning around Jupiter for hundreds of years.

The Sun's atmosphere

Stars have atmospheres, too. Our Sun is a star. The Sun's dazzling brightness normally makes it impossible to see its atmosphere. But when the Sun is hidden behind the **Moon**, its atmosphere becomes visible.

Moon gases

Moons do not hold on to an atmosphere. They are too small. Their **gravity** is too weak. But there is one exception. Titan, a moon of Saturn, has a thick atmosphere.

Harsh weather on Earth can easily be spotted from space.

Why do the planets look so different from each other?

Earth looks like a blue ball hanging in space. This is because 70 percent of its surface is covered with water. Venus looks whitish-yellow. This is because of sunlight reflected (sent back) by its thick **atmosphere**.

Earth looks blue because it is covered with water.

Mars looks red. This is because it is covered with a thin layer of dust. This contains **iron oxide** (a substance made of the **elements oxygen** and iron)—also known as rust! Mercury looks gray-brown. This is the color of its bare, rocky surface.

The atmospheres of the **gas giants** are made mainly of **hydrogen** and **helium gas**. But small amounts of other gases produce their different colors. Jupiter is red, orange, and white. Saturn is yellow. Uranus is blue-green. Neptune is blue.

Stripes and rings

Jupiter is covered with bold stripes. They are bands of clouds.

All four of the gas planets have rings around them. Jupiter, Uranus, and Neptune have rings that are difficult to see. Their rings are thin, dark, and dusty. Saturn's rings are by far the biggest and brightest. They are bright because they are made almost entirely of ice. Ice reflects sunlight well.

Saturn looks different from all the other planets. This is because it is the only planet that is surrounded by bright rings.

Orbit, Spin, and Tilt

It does not feel as though Earth is moving. But it is actually moving very fast! Earth and all the planets constantly move, in several different ways.

Orbit

Earth **orbits** the Sun at a speed of about 108,000 kilometers (67,100 miles) per hour. Like all the planets, Earth travels around the Sun in a counterclockwise direction (the opposite direction of a clock).

Earth takes 365.25 days to orbit the Sun. This gives us the length of our year. Planets closer to the Sun orbit faster. The planet Mercury takes only 88 Earth-days to orbit the Sun. Planets farther away orbit more slowly. Neptune, the farthest planet from the Sun, takes 165 Earth-years to orbit the Sun.

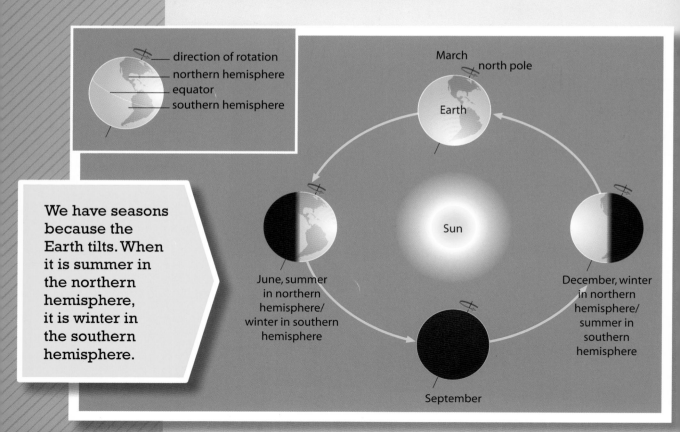

direction of rotation
northern hemisphere
equator
southern hemisphere

March
north pole
Earth

Sun

We have seasons because the Earth tilts. When it is summer in the northern hemisphere, it is winter in the southern hemisphere.

June, summer in northern hemisphere/ winter in southern hemisphere

December, winter in northern hemisphere/ summer in southern hemisphere

September

The planet Uranus tilts four times more than Earth. It lies on its side.

Tilt and seasons

Earth's tilt produces the seasons. For part of the year, the northern half of Earth, called the **northern hemisphere**, tilts toward the Sun. This brings spring and summer to countries there. As Earth continues around the Sun, the northern hemisphere tilts away from the Sun. It cools down. This brings fall and winter. The southern half of Earth, or **southern hemisphere**, then tilts in the direction of the Sun. It has spring and summer.

Spin and tilt

All the planets spin. Earth spins once about every 24 hours. This gives us the length of a day. When the planets formed, they all spun in the same direction. Today, Venus spins in the opposite direction. Its spin might have been reversed by crashing into something else.

All of the planets tilt. They look like toy spinning tops leaning over. Some tilt more than others. Earth's tilt creates the seasons. (See the box, at right, and the art, at left.)

The Sun is blotted out during a total solar eclipse.

A Sun-eating dragon?

Today, we know why solar eclipses happen. But in the past, people did not understand why the Sun suddenly disappeared. A solar eclipse was feared. Some people believed that a dragon was trying to eat the Sun!

Eclipses

The **Moon orbits** Earth. Earth orbits the Sun. As this happens, the three bodies sometimes line up together. This leads to two possible results.

The first result is a **solar eclipse**. This happens when the Moon passes between Earth and the Sun. If the Moon passes in front of the Sun, it casts a shadow on Earth. Depending on where they are standing, some people on Earth see a total eclipse. The Sun disappears behind the Moon. Other people see a partial eclipse. The Moon passes in front of part of the Sun. The Sun looks as if someone has taken a bite out of it.

WORD STATION

lunar eclipse darkening of the Moon when it travels through Earth's shadow

The second result is a **lunar eclipse**. This happens when the Moon moves into Earth's shadow. But the Moon does not disappear. Instead, it turns red!

This is because Earth's **atmosphere** bends the Sun's light. This light travels around Earth and onto the Moon. There are different colors in this sunlight. The red part of sunlight is able to travel through the atmosphere and onto the Moon. For this reason, the Moon looks red.

The Moon turns red during a lunar eclipse.

Moons and Their Effects

Moon rocks rock!

Scientists used to wonder where the Moon came from. They found the answer when **astronauts** landed on the Moon. They brought Moon rocks back to Earth. The Moon rocks were found to be the same as rock on Earth's surface. This shows that the Moon must have formed out of rock from Earth.

A **moon** is made of rock. It **orbits** a larger body, such as a planet. The planets Mercury and Venus have no moons. Earth has one large moon, called the Moon. Mars has two tiny moons, called Phobos and Deimos. The four **gas giant** planets each have dozens of moons.

Making moons

Most moons were once chunks of rock. These rocks were wandering through the **solar system**. Then they were caught by the **gravity** of the planets they now orbit.

Earth's Moon is different. At first, Earth had no moon. Then, about 4.45 billion years ago, a planet-sized body crashed into Earth. Parts of both objects blasted out into space. All the bits and pieces eventually collected, forming the Moon.

Changing shapes

The same side of the Moon always faces Earth. But the part we can see at night changes shape. Over time, we see more of the Moon's sunlit half every night. Then, we see the whole sunlit half. This is the full Moon. Then, we see less and less of it every night. It then disappears altogether. This is the new Moon.

The shape of the Moon changes from night to night. This is caused by the changing positions of Earth and the Moon as they travel around the Sun.

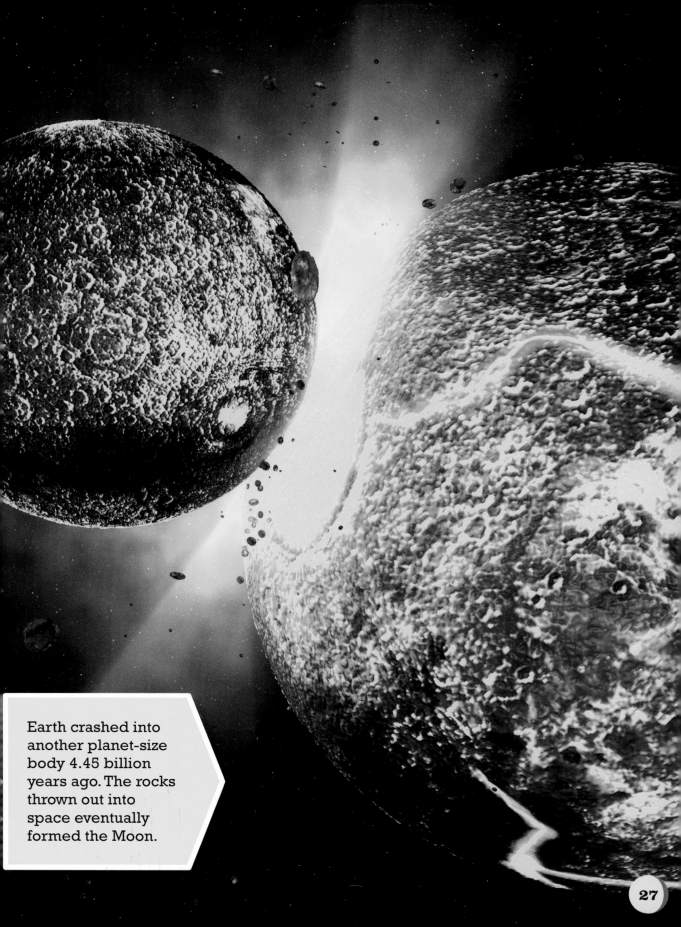

Earth crashed into another planet-size body 4.45 billion years ago. The rocks thrown out into space eventually formed the Moon.

Steady now

Without the Moon, we wouldn't be here! The Moon steadies Earth's spin. It stops it from wobbling. Without the steadying effect of the Moon, Earth's weather would not stay the same in one place. This would have prevented complex life from developing.

What do moons do?

Moons are tiny compared to the planets they **orbit**. But they sometimes have important effects on the planets.

Earth's Moon has a major effect. Twice a day, the ocean washes up higher onto the shore and then falls back again. These events are called **high tides**. The Moon's **gravity** pulls the ocean toward it. A swollen bulge of water piles up on the Moon's side of Earth. A smaller bulge of water is left behind on the opposite side of Earth. As Earth spins, the two bulges try to stay in line with the Moon. The sea level rises as each bulge of water sweeps past and then falls again.

Saturn's rings have gaps in them. These gaps were caused by moons. The moons' gravity pulled away tiny pieces in the rings, forming the gaps.

WORD STATION
high tide rise in sea levels caused by the pull of the Moon's gravity

Volcanic Io

Planets also affect moons. One of the most amazing effects is seen on one of Jupiter's moons, Io. Jupiter's powerful gravity pulls and crushes Io as it orbits Jupiter. This produces hundreds of volcanoes on Io's surface.

This shows Jupiter's moon, Io. The black, brown, green, orange, and red spots on its surface mark the locations of volcanoes. Computers changed the colors to make them stand out.

Downsizing Pluto

Until 2005 Pluto was called a planet. In 2005 reports announced the discovery of a tenth planet in the **solar system** called Eris. Eris was similar to two other bodies that had already been discovered. Scientist had to decide whether to call these bodies "planets." They decide to call them "**dwarf planets**." They kept the name "planet" for a few special bodies. Since Pluto was similar to Eris, Pluto was now called a dwarf planet. This changed the number of planets in the solar system from nine to eight.

Discovering the Solar System

Ancient scientists knew of the first six planets, from Mercury to Saturn. These planets can be seen with the human eye. The rest of the planets were not discovered until the **telescope** was invented. The telescope allowed people to look deeper into space than ever before.

In 1609 the Italian astronomer Galileo Galilei looked at the night sky through a telescope.

Hunting planets

In 1781 an **astronomer** (scientist who studies space) named Sir William Herschel turned his telescope to the sky. He noticed a speck of light moving. It was the planet Uranus.

Astronomers found that Uranus was not moving exactly as they thought it should. They wondered if another planet could be tugging Uranus out of position. Mathematicians (experts at math) figured out where the other planet should be. In 1846 astronomers found it. This planet was Neptune.

In 1930 Clyde Tombaugh discovered Pluto. This was once considered a planet (see box on page 30.) It took him over a year of studying photographs to find it.

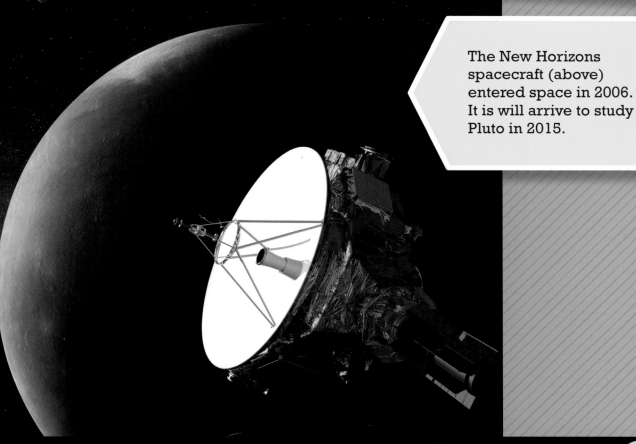

The New Horizons spacecraft (above) entered space in 2006. It is will arrive to study Pluto in 2015.

Looking for life

There is life almost everywhere we look on Earth. But what about the rest of the **solar system**? Life on Earth needs two things: water and **energy**. Water is plentiful on Earth. Energy is supplied by the Sun. Planets closer to the Sun are too hot for liquid water. Planets farther away are too cold. Until recently, life was thought to be possible only within a narrow area of space around the Sun. This narrow area is known as the Goldilocks zone.

In the news

Are the real Martians worms?

On August 6, 1996, a **meteorite** (piece of rock) that fell from Mars made front-page news all over the world. Some scientists who studied it found worm-like shapes inside the rock. They thought these might be signs of life on Mars. But since then, other scientists have shown that the "worms" are not related to life on Mars. It seems that life on Mars had not been discovered after all.

Could these worm-like shapes be the remains of living things that once lived on Mars? Most scientists now think that the shapes are not evidence of life on Mars.

WORD STATION
meteorite large rock that enters the atmosphere and survives its fall

Jupiter's **moon**, Europa, has an icy surface. This may cover an ocean of water. Wherever there is water on Earth, there is life. So, there may be life on Europa, too.

Where are the Martians?

In the past, some people thought intelligent creatures lived on the planet Mars. But when spacecraft visited Mars, they found no life. Although it once had water, Mars is a dry, dusty world today.

Extreme life

Scientists explored Earth's ocean floor in the 1970s. They were amazed to discover rocks covered with snails, crabs, giant worms, and other creatures. The question was: Without sunlight, where did their energy come from?

The creatures crowd around hot springs (warm flows of water) beneath the ocean floor. Tiny living things called **bacteria** get energy from substances in the water. These bacteria and other living things are food for larger life-forms there. This has made scientists rethink life on other planets. If life can exist in a place like this on Earth, maybe it could exist in other places, too.

Space Rocks

As the **solar system** formed, billions of pieces of rock and ice did not become part of the Sun, planets, or **moons**. Many of them are still flying around the solar system today.

Hale-Bopp was the brightest comet of the 1990s.

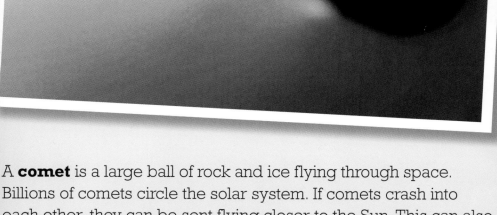

The Giotto spacecraft took photographs of Halley's Comet. They showed a huge mountain of dark dust and big pieces of ice.

Halley's Comet

The **orbits** of some comets bring them back to our part of the solar system again and again. One of these, Halley's Comet, comes back every 76 years. In 1986, as the comet neared the Sun, the European Space Agency sent the Giotto spacecraft to meet it. Giotto took photographs. These photographs showed that comets are made of rock and ice.

A **comet** is a large ball of rock and ice flying through space. Billions of comets circle the solar system. If comets crash into each other, they can be sent flying closer to the Sun. This can also happen if the **gravity** of a passing star has a pull.

As a comet nears the Sun, it warms up. Some of its ice changes to **gas**. Gas and dust coming off a comet stretch out into two long tails—a gas tail and a dust tail. Most comets can only be seen clearly by looking at them through a **telescope**. Every 10 years or so, a comet big enough and bright enough to be seen with the human eye appears in the sky.

From time to time, an asteroid passes close to Earth. In the distant past, asteroids actually hit Earth. One that hit Earth 65 million years ago may have helped end the period when dinosaurs lived on Earth.

Points of light

Asteroids were once thought to look like stars. But they are actually pieces of rock that **orbit** the Sun like planets. Most asteroids are less than 1.6 kilometers (1 mile) across. Nearly all of them are found in a wide area between the orbits of Mars and Jupiter. This area is called the **asteroid belt**. Some asteroids are big enough to have their own **moons**.

If a huge asteroid ever hits Earth, it might look something like this. Several groups scan the skies. They search for any asteroid or **comet** that might crash into Earth.

WORD STATION

asteroid large body made of rock found mainly in the asteroid belt

Asteroid Ida has its own tiny moon, called Dactyl.

Dactyl

Ida

Where did they come from?

In the early **solar system**, the asteroid belt contained many large pieces of rock. They failed to come together to form a planet. This was because of Jupiter's **gravity**. This force pulled on the rocks and caused them to crash violently into each other. These crashes broke up the rocks. This formed the billions of asteroids that we see today.

What is a shooting star?

Rocks in space that are smaller than 10 meters (33 feet) are called **meteoroids**. If a meteoroid as small as a grain of sand flies into Earth's **atmosphere**, it heats up very quickly. It glows for a fraction of a second before burning up completely. This makes a streak of light called a **meteor**. Meteors are also known as shooting stars. Sometimes Earth passes through a trail left behind by a passing **comet**. The result can be a display of shooting stars called a **meteor shower**.

Some meteoroids are big enough to fly all the way through the atmosphere and land on Earth. These are called **meteorites**. A large meteorite makes a hole in the ground called a crater.

This 1,200-meter (3,940-foot) crater is in the state of Arizona. It was made about 50,000 years ago by a huge meteorite.

WORD STATION
meteor streak of light when a meteoroid enters Earth's atmosphere

This basketball-sized rock was discovered on Mars. It was the first meteorite ever found on another planet.

Mars rocks

When the **Moon** and other planets are hit by meteorites, the crashes are sometimes very powerful. They send rock flying out from the surface—all the way into space. A few of these rocks from the Moon and Mars have landed on Earth.

Meteorites on Mars

In 2005 newspapers announced that scientists had discovered a rock on Mars that might be a meteorite. Tests show that it is indeed a meteorite.

Looking into the Future

The **solar system** will not last forever. This is because the Sun will not last forever. A few billion years from now, the Sun will run out of **energy**. The dying Sun will grow bigger and turn red. It will change into a star called a **red giant**. It will swallow the planets Mercury and Venus, and probably Earth. Then the Sun will shrink and become a tiny, cool star.

A lifeless Earth

Long before the Sun turns into a red giant, most life on Earth will become impossible. The **Moon** is moving farther away from Earth. Within two billion years, the Moon will be so far away that it will no longer steady Earth's tilt. Earth will wobble so much as it spins that most of the life on Earth will end.

The Sun will change into a red giant star like this in a few billion years.

Earth's hot **core** is cooling down. When the liquid part of the core cools down enough, it will become solid. It will no longer produce a **magnetic field**. Without this field, the **solar wind** will affect Earth. It will sweep our **atmosphere** away into space.

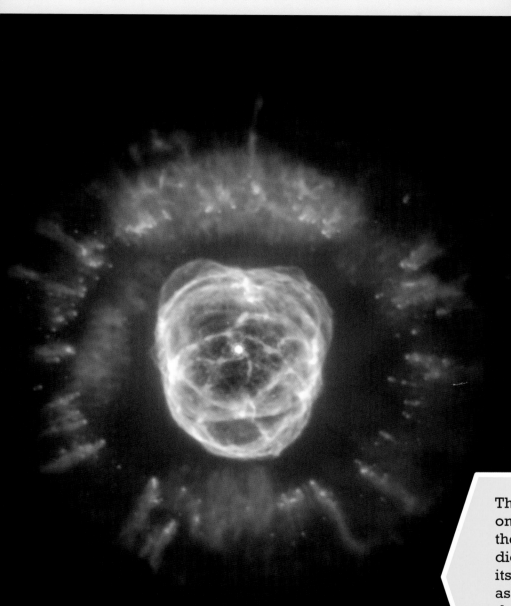

This **nebula** was once a star like the Sun. As it died, it threw off its outer layers, as the Sun will do. This formed the patterns that surround it here.

Timeline of Space Exploration Missions

The following is a timeline of just some of the most important space **missions**:

1950s

Date	Mission	Description
Oct. 4, 1957	Sputnik 1	first human-made **satellite** to go into **orbit** around Earth
Jan. 2, 1959	Luna 1	first spacecraft to fly past the **Moon**
Oct. 7, 1959	Luna 3	took the first photographs of the far side of the Moon

1960s

Date	Mission	Description
Apr. 12, 1961	Vostok 1	carried Yuri Gagarin, the first person to orbit Earth
Jan. 31, 1966	Luna 9	first Moon lander (vehicle that lands on a planet)
Dec. 21, 1968	Apollo 8	first spacecraft with **astronauts** to orbit the Moon
July 20, 1969	Apollo 11	first landing with astronauts on the Moon

1970s

Date	Mission	Description
Sept. 12, 1970	Luna 16	first sample returned from the Moon
May 19, 1971	Mars 2	first spacecraft to land on Mars
May 30, 1971	Mariner 9	first spacecraft to orbit another planet (Mars)
Aug. 12, 1978	ISEE-3	studied the effect of the **solar wind** on Earth's **magnetic field**; also the first spacecraft to fly past a **comet**

1980s

Date	Mission	Description
Apr. 12, 1981	Columbia	first launch of the U.S. space shuttle
July 2, 1985	Giotto	flew past Halley's Comet
Oct. 18, 1989	Galileo	first **asteroid** fly-by; first exploration of Jupiter's **atmosphere**

1990s

Date	Mission	Description
Apr. 24, 1990	Hubble Space Telescope	orbital space **telescope**
Dec. 2, 1995	SOHO	launch of the Solar and Heliospheric Observatory (SOHO) to study the Sun and space weather
Feb. 17, 1996	NEAR	first spacecraft to fly past, orbit, and land on a near-Earth asteroid
Dec. 4, 1996	Mars pathfinder	landed the first rover (called Sojourner) on Mars. A rover is a vehicle that travels across the surface of a planet.

Date	Mission	Description
Oct. 15, 1997	Cassini-Huygens	first spacecraft to orbit Saturn; also landed a small spacecraft on Titan, one of Saturn's moons
Nov. 20, 1998	International Space Station	launch of first part of the International Space Station

2000s

Date	Mission	Description
Aug. 8, 2001	Genesis	first spacecraft to collect **particles** of the solar wind
June 10, 2003 July 7, 2003	Spirit and Opportunity	rovers arrived on Mars in 2004
Mar. 2, 2004	Rosetta	due to meet up with comet Churyumov-Gerasimenko in 2014, Rosetta will orbit the comet and put a lander (a space vehicle that lands on the surface) on it
Jan. 19, 2006	New Horizons	will be the first spacecraft to do a close-up study of Pluto, due to reach Pluto in 2015

Planets: The Vital Statistics

	Distance from Sun	Diameter	Number of moons	Length of day (sunrise to sunrise)
Mercury	58 million km	4,880 km	0	176 Earth-days
Venus	108 million km	12,104 km	0	117 Earth-days
Earth	150 million km	12,756 km	1	24 hours
Mars	228 million km	6,794 km	2	24.6 hours
Jupiter	779 million km	143,000 km	63	9.8 hours
Saturn	1.4 billion km	120,000 km	60*	10.2 hours
Uranus	2.9 billion km	51,120 km	27	17.2 hours
Neptune	4.5 billion km	49,530 km	13	16.1 hours

More moons are still being discovered around the **gas giants**. By the year 2000, only 18 of Jupiter's moons were known. By 2003 more than 40 more had been discovered. More are likely to be discovered in the future.

*The exact number of Saturn's moons is unclear, but it is usually listed as at least 60.

Glossary

asteroid body made of rock bigger than about 10 meters (33 feet) across, found mainly in the asteroid belt

asteroid belt wide area with asteroids between the orbits of Mars and Jupiter

astronaut person who travels to space in a spacecraft

astronomer scientist who studies stars

atmosphere layer of gases that surrounds a planet

atom tiny building block that makes up elements

aurora glowing, colored light in the sky caused by particles from the Sun crashing into gas in the atmosphere

bacterium (more than one: "bacteria") very small, simple life-form

comet ball of rock and ice that develops a bright tail or tails when it nears the Sun

core center

crust planet's outermost layer of rock

dense full of material

dwarf planet large body in space that orbits the Sun, but is not large enough to be a major planet

element simplest type of substance that exists

energy ability to do work

gas substance with no definite shape, like air

gas giant one of the four planets in the solar system farthest from the Sun

gravity pull that a large object has on a smaller one nearby. Gravity holds the solar system together.

helium element in the form of a colorless, odorless gas

high tide rise in sea levels caused by the pull of the Moon's gravity

hydrogen element in gas form that is the most plentiful element in the universe. It helps make up the Sun.

iron oxide substance made of the elements oxygen and iron, also known as rust

lunar eclipse darkening of the Moon caused when the Moon travels through Earth's shadow

magnetic behaving like a magnet

magnetic field effect of a magnet on the area around it

mantle hot, liquid rock layer of an Earth-like planet that lies between its core and its crust

meteor streak of light seen in the sky, caused by a meteoroid entering Earth's atmosphere and heating up

meteorite meteoroid that enters the atmosphere from space and survives its fall

meteoroid piece of rock up to about 10 meters (33 feet) across traveling through space in orbit around the Sun

meteor shower large number of meteors seen when Earth travels through dust left behind by a comet

moon small natural body made of rock that orbits a planet

nebula (more than one: "nebulae") cloud of dust and gas, mainly hydrogen, in space

nitrogen element in the form of a colorless, odorless gas that helps make up Earth's atmosphere

northern hemisphere northern half of Earth

nuclear fusion joining of atoms under pressure, releasing huge amounts of energy

orbit circle around something, such as a planet

oxygen element in gas form that helps make up Earth's atmosphere. We need oxygen to breathe.

particle tiny piece of material

plate section

prominence tongue of gas curling out into space above the Sun

protoplanet body about the same size as the Moon that grows by attracting more gas and dust, until it becomes a planet

red giant huge, bright-red star that is very old

rocky planet one of the planets in the solar system closest to the Sun

satellite object that orbits, or circles around, a planet

solar eclipse event that occurs when the Moon passes between the Sun and Earth, casting a shadow on Earth

solar system our Sun and its family of planets and all other objects that orbit (circle) around it

solar wind constant stream of particles flying out of the Sun in all directions

southern hemisphere northern half of Earth

supernova (more than one: "supernovae") explosive death of a star

telescope instrument that makes distant objects appear much bigger and nearer

troposphere lowest layer of Earth's atmosphere, where we experience weather

universe space and everything in it

Find Out More

Books

Couper, Heather, and Nigel Henbest. *DK Encyclopedia of Space.* New York: Dorling Kindersley, 2009.

Farndon, John. *Exploring the Solar System.* Chicago: Heinemann Library, 2008.

Grego, Peter. *Discovering the Solar System.* North Mankato, Minn.: QEB, 2007.

Harris, Joseph. *Space Exploration: Impact of Science and Technology.* Pleasantville, N.Y.: Gareth Stevens, 2010.

Jefferis, David. *Space Probes: Exploring Beyond Earth.* New York: Crabtree, 2009.

Stott, Carole. *Space Exploration.* New York: Dorling Kindersley, 2010.

Trammel, Howard K. *The Solar System.* New York: Children's Press, 2010.

Websites

http://sse.jpl.nasa.gov/kids/index.cfm
The website of NASA, the U.S. space agency, offers fun things to read and do.

http://spaceplace.jpl.nasa.gov/en/kids/mars_rocket.shtml
Go on a mission to Mars.

http://solarsystem.jpl.nasa.gov/planets/index.cfm
Find out more about the planets and their moons.

www.esa.int/esaKIDSen/LifeinSpace.html
Find out more about space exploration and life in space.

Places to visit

Smithsonian National Air and Space Museum

Independence Ave at 6th Street, SW
Washington, D.C. 20560
www.nasm.si.edu

This museum is full of examples of technology and photos from the history of space flight.

John F. Kennedy Space Center

Kennedy Space Center, Florida 32899
www.kennedyspacecenter.com

While visiting the Kennedy Space Center, you may be able to witness the launch of a spacecraft.

Topics to investigate

Extraterrestrial life

Life may have developed on other planets or moons differently from life on Earth. What might life on other planets or moons look like?

The cost of exploration

Is the exploration of the solar system worth the cost? It costs millions of dollars to send a space probe to visit a planet. Space exploration with astronauts costs billions of dollars.

Space weather

The changing conditions in space near Earth are known as space weather. The weather in space can affect satellites and spacecraft with astronauts orbiting Earth. Electronic systems in spacecraft can be damaged, and astronauts' lives may be at risk.

Index

3 1901 05221 0996